50 INVENTION IDEAS FOR STARTUPS

GET AN IDEA, START A BUSINESS

VICTOR BORAH

ISBN 979-888591934-0

In loving memory of my Papa

Late Umesh Borah

You wanted me to be an inventor
Perhaps, I couldn't be one,
May be, InA far corner of this world,
'Someone
Might follow my dreams
And make you happy
And the world..
A better place to live in.

Contents

Contents

Contents

Foreword

This book is meant for the inventor who is passionate about making big money and a fame for himself.

From Agriculture to Pets, from Household Utilities to Workplaces, this book covers 50 possible inventions that are yet to rock the world.

Some of the ideas seem to be funny but very interesting and feasible to be done, others are serious and are equally doable too.

These ideas occurred to me in a span of a few years and out of several hundreds of those ideas, many have already seen the light of mass production. My family would frequently react to such gadgets and tell me, "*Hey, your dream machine has been invented elsewhere, when will you put your ideas to use*?" – I just smile.

Might be, you can get your next great idea from me and you owe me nothing besides purchasing this little book. The entire invention and the possible profits are yours to keep!

Also, don't worry, I have the best inventions up my sleeve and for myself, (grin).

So, why wait, get your favorite invention out to your workbench, work on it, build a prototype, patent it, market it and make tons of money. Now, hurry up.. It's getting late by the day!

Happy Inventing,

Victor Borah

Preface

50 Invention Ideas for Startups: written by Victor Vashkar Borah is a collection of 50 ideas to invent electromechanical programmable smart devices for homes, offices, factories, farming lands and other utility devices. The inventions involves technologies from different fields of engineering like Electronics, IoT, Machine Learning, Artificial Intelligence and Chemical Engineering with requirements for Mechanical Actuations too. With ideas from this book, you can start your next great invention. You are free to copy ideas from this book use them in your next big project and earn money from your invention. The sooner you read this book and grab an idea, the sooner you get the next successful patent. So, why waste time, read this book now. your time starts now!

What you can do: copy ideas from this book and use them in your projects as your own. Apply for patents based on ideas from this book, improve those ideas and then claim for patents.

What you cannot do: you cannot copy any content from this book, put it in another publication, physically or digitally, as image or text and claim as your own creation or resell parts of this book without the author's prior written permission.

victorborah@gmail.com

Acknowledgements

Sincere gratitude to my family for letting me put my ideas together in the form of a book and make it available to the world. I thank my family for believing in me and supporting me in every aspect of my life and helping me put this book out.

CHAPTER ONE

The Idea: Windowpane cleaning device

Difficulty: **Moderate**

The Problem: It is difficult to reach & clean window glasses and most of the devices available are not that effective

Specifications:

Design 1: The device can be a robotic remote-operated window glass cleaning machine that can be controlled through an app on the smartphone and can be installed very easily to one's home through the windows.

Design 2: Make a Self-Cleaning window that already has the device installed, just like the wipers of a windshield. The function will be the same as a wiper set but with the exception of adding cleaning agents and detergents.

Things to keep in mind:

1. The user must be able to interact with the device through his smartphone.
2. The cleaning materials must not drip to the ground or elsewhere.
3. The status of the cleaning agents must be tracked and notified through the app.
4. The status of whether the glass needs cleaning or not must be diagnosed and notified to the user through the app just as an anti-virus software prompts a user to clean his device.
5. An automatic cleaning feature will come in handy.

CHAPTER TWO

The Idea: Device to scan a farming field for pests

Difficulty: **Difficult**

The Problem: Pests in a farming field lead to huge losses every year around the world and no invention exists that can put an end to this misery.

Specifications:

The device must be such that it can be installed in a farming field, and possibly outdoors. The device must have the capability to scan and detect the presence of pests such as rodents, snakes, locusts, beetles, crickets, and other bugs. It must have some sort of sensor or camera that will have the ability to scan the field and the crops for pests and match them with a predefined database and then send alerts and notifications to the owners on the kind of pest present and the damage it has already done or potential damage that it can do.

Things to keep in mind:

1. The device must be able to scan a large area, possibly like an acre of land or more.
2. The device can have a network of sensors as nodes to collect data from the location.
3. The device must be designed for use outdoors and must have the capability to stand the common natural elements such as rain, heat, snow, etc.
4. The device must be capable of attaching to a mobile app through the internet which will then produce required reports and notifications.

CHAPTER THREE

The Idea: Make a device to keep records and track all contents of a packed suitcase

Difficulty: **Difficult**

The Problem: While traveling, we often tend to forget our belongings before checking out from a hotel.

Specifications:

Make an artificially intelligent device that can see what things we are putting into a suitcase. It will be accompanied by a companion app that we can use to see what things we have put into the suitcase. Once we confirm, the things that we have entered, it will then monitor the changes that we have done to the contents during our trip and notify us, if we miss putting something in again after a while.

Things to keep in mind:

1. The device must be able to detect and differentiate between "Putting-Things-Inside" and "Taking-Things-Out" actions.
2. The device must be able to recognize objects through cameras and sensors aided by Artificial Intelligence. Like, it will be able to "see" things like shirts, Trousers, diaries, Pen, etc.
3. The device will communicate through a companion app that will present the user with a list of the possible contents which the user will then rectify to his satisfaction and confirm the package.

CHAPTER FOUR

The Idea: Make a device to obtain tire information of one's car

Difficulty: **Moderate**

The Problem: We have to manually check the condition of the tires of our car including air pressure.

Specifications:

Make a device that can automatically get the "Tire Information" from a car. Vital information like Tire Pressure, Tire Temperature, etc. must be obtained electronically and notified to the user.

Things to keep in mind:

1. We must be able to install the device to any model and make of car.
2. The device must implement some ingenious contact-less method of obtaining the data for a particular wheel.
3. The device must be able to withstand severe outdoor driving conditions.
4. The driver must be notified through some dashboard or external mechanism in case of serious or issues that have to be looked into immediately while driving.
5. The device must have the capability to be connected to the internet to a cloud server for further storage and retrieval of the wheel data

CHAPTER FIVE

The Idea: Make a smart electronic face mask to detect air quality

Difficulty: **Moderate**

The Problem: Conventional face masks do not have smart features such as detecting the level of pollution.

Specifications:

Make a wearable electronic face mask that can obtain environmental parameters such as Oxygen Level, Air Pressure, Levels of other gasses in the air and if possible, provide electronically balanced air.

Things to keep in mind:

1. The mask must be wearable without any physical discomfort.
2. The mask can have a tiny battery included that can power the system.
3. The mask can have the ability to pair with a mobile app to produce reports and statistics.
4. The mask can notify the user through the smartphone in case it detects harmful levels of gases in the air. That will be very handy for people working in hazardous situations.
5. The mobile app can have a cloud service that can track the user's air-environments that he had been to and then produce a health graph based on the air that he has inhaled in the past.

CHAPTER SIX

The Idea: Make a device to check if the rains are acidic or not

Difficulty: **Difficult**

The Problem: Acid rains are turning to be a man-made hazard in areas nearby to industrial sectors. A machine that can detect the presence of levels of harmful chemicals in the rainwater can save lives, crops, and buildings.

Specifications:

Make a device that we can install in hour homes. The device will be able to collect rainwater, analyze it through sensors connected to it and then process the information and present it to the user.

Things to keep in mind:

1. The Device must be able to detect the maximum harmful chemical that will include, Sulphur, Chlorine, Bromine, and other industrial chemicals.
2. The more chemicals it can detect, the more useful it will be.
3. The device might have accompanying software that can be accessed from a PC to get more information and get in-depth charts and graphs.
4. The device might carry chemically designed probes that might require legal permissions as per the location it is meant to be used in.
5. The device must have the ability to send out real-time notifications to its users in case of serious issues.

CHAPTER SEVEN

The Idea: Make an automated robotic submarine that will capture fish

Difficulty: **Difficult**

The Problem: Fishinghad always carried its own problems and dangers. It had never been safe to go out into the sea and catch fish.

Specifications:

Make a “Robotic Submarine” that can go out into the sea and catch fish just like a trawler. It will have a bin and a system to catch fish and put them into the bin. It will then send the data to its owner and rise to the surface with the catch.

Things to keep in mind:

1. The Device must be able to be used in lakes and the seas alike.
2. The device must have its own onboard power source.
3. The device must have the capability to communicate with its owner, just like a spacecraft is controlled by mission control.
4. The owner and his team must be able to evaluate the catch inside the device storage.
5. The owner must have the ability to release the catch at any moment or to fetch it to the surface.

CHAPTER EIGHT

The Idea: Make cloth-line machine

Difficulty: **Easy**

The Problem: Most of us dry our clothes in the sunshine that is hung from a cloth line. The issue is, everything is perfect until it rains.

Specifications:

Make an "Automatic Cloth-Line Manger" machine that will fetch all my cloth from the outdoor cloth line and put them inside as soon as it starts raining.

Things to keep in mind:

1. The device must have the capability of installing outdoors.
2. The device must have some sort of input data on the weather. It can be through weather API, External sensors, or whatever.
3. The device must be able to put the clothes out again, once the sky is clear, without manual human intervention.
4. The device should be able to communicate with the user through a mobile app, in case it rains or if the sky is clear, and the cloth is out again.
5. The device must have the ability to put the lot in again after a specific period of time, like before sunset. That will mean a 100% sense of peace for the homemaker.

CHAPTER NINE

The Idea: Design a Book Dispensing machine for the Physical Paper Books Library

Difficulty: **Very Difficult**

The Problem: It's difficult for a library operator to fetch a physical paper book out from a shelf from among millions of books out there. Also, monitoring books is a big issue.

Specifications:

Make an "Automatic Book Storage and fetching" machine that will store, organize and fetch books at the click of a button from some sort of physical "Books-Bin". The Machine will be accompanied by a Library Management System that will provide user Interfaces and databases and a system to track, record, and organize the books into those bins.

Things to keep in mind:

1. There can be millions of Books in a large library.
2. We can start with a simple system that stores and dispenses say a hundred books. Combining many of these will produce a large system.
3. There must be proper software to run the system.
4. There must be a mechanical storage system that will include "Putting a Book In" & "Extracting a Book Out".
5. It doesn't matter where the book is stored physically, it will always be dispensed through a common slot, preferably at the counter.

CHAPTER TEN

The Idea: Make a portable and handy device to test food contamination in hotels & restaurants

Difficulty: **Difficult**

The Problem: We eat food in hotels and restaurants purely based on trust and faith. Never had we any way of finding out, the levels of contamination in the food served.

Specifications:

Make a portable hand-held device to test food. We might be able to dip it into a food sample or put a food sample into it. It will have chemical sensors that will have the ability to detect adulteration in the food sample. Once the test is over, the device will then produce the reports and produce it through an app I the smartphone.

Things to keep in mind:

1. The device must be small enough to be carried in a backup and fetch it whenever we deem it fit that the food must be tested.
2. The device must have its own power source that can be charged just like any other device
3. The device must have a companion app that can be used to generate reports of the food it has tested
4. Through the companion app, we might be able to fetch external that is relevant data to the analysis.

5. In case of detection of harmful substances, the device must be able to produce alarms and notifications.

CHAPTER ELEVEN

The Idea: Make a device with an app to detect the presence of wild animals near a camping area

Difficulty: **VeryDifficult**

The Problem: While camping outdoors in a seemingly beautiful and safe location, we are always in danger of predators lurking in the dark. There must be a machine to scan the area and find if any danger is out there.

Specifications:

Make a machine that can scan the area near a campsite like radar and find what wild animals are lurking in the dark. The device might also accompany a drone with sensors to fly and scan a particular area.

Things to keep in mind:

1. The device must be small enough to be carried in a backup to a campsite.
2. The device must use as little power as possible so that it becomes jungle-friendly.
3. If there is a companion drone, then the device must be able to extract data from it conveniently.
4. On detection of any danger, the device must be able to specify what sort of danger it is.
5. The machine must be able to detect both reptiles and quadrupeds.

CHAPTER TWELVE

The Idea: Make a Gift packing machine for use in homes

Difficulty: **Moderate**

The Problem: We always have to manually wrap gift paper around a gift and it takes some time to learn how to wrap a gift perfectly. It is quite tedious to wrap a lot of gifts this way, especially during Christmas.

Specifications:

Make a machine that can wrap a Gift-Paper around a gift with labels and ribbons complete.

Things to keep in mind:

1. There must be a compartment to load rolls of gift paper.
2. The machine will pull the gift paper from the roll and wrap it mechanically around the present.
3. It will also stick labels, stickers and also tie a ribbon with a knot around the gift if required.
4. Once done, it will beep a sound to let the user know, that the job is done.
5. We can provide the option of loading different gift-paper sizes for presents of variable sizes.

CHAPTER THIRTEEN

The Idea: Make an origami machine

Difficulty: **Difficult**

The Problem: origami had always been a difficult yet majestic art. People have always struggled to learn it with perfection. Why not make an origami machine that can teach how to fold a piece of paper and create masterpieces.

Specifications:

A machine with fingers and turntables that can fold paper into the subtle art of origami. An LCD connected to the device will let users choose what design he needs. Once selected, the machine will proceed with tutorials sounding off and then folding the paper.

Things to keep in mind:

1. The machine must have a display unit that presents users with a menu to pick their design.
2. The machine will have a "Teach & Train" mode that will demonstrate the design in steps that are displayed on the screen and with sounds that elaborate what to do now.
3. We might be able to download new designs to the machine from the internet.
4. Paper damage must be minimal.
5. Different sizes can be integrated into the machine.

CHAPTER FOURTEEN

The Idea: Make a robotic dolphin to teach kids how to swim

Difficulty: **VeryDifficult**

The Problem: Teaching kids how to swim, has always been very difficult. We need expert trainers for that. How about making such as a device that can carry children and teach them how to swim?

Specifications:

A machine with life-support such as floating mechanism, anti-skid protection, etc. to teach kids to swim. Put a kid into the dolphin. There is water inside the dolphin's inner but also, there are actuators inside that will actually move the kid's body in the water. The machine will glide through the swimming pool like a dolphin and the kid will mimic the movement of the actuators.

Things to keep in mind:

1. The machine must be safe enough to put a kid into it.
2. The machine must have gyro sensing and detect when the kid is going to tumble over or when he is unable to make any move.
3. The machine can be monitored through computers connected to it.
4. The machine must have its own power supply.
5. The machine must have the option to be controlled by swimming aides beside the device in the pool.

CHAPTER FIFTEEN

The Idea: Make a Posture correction device

Difficulty: **Difficult**

The Problem: Posture is one issue that most of the people around the globe are affected by. We suffer from pain and also undergo, tissue, bone, and cartilage damage due to the wrong posture of our body, often while working.

Specifications:

A machine that can detect our body posture and trigger an alarm or a notification when it finds the posture to be unhealthy.

Things to keep in mind:

1. The device must be able to detect several postures that may include actions such as walking, sitting, sleeping, running, etc.
2. The device must be able to send notifications through a health app in our smartphone.
3. The device must have the option to send beeps to the user notifying of an extended wrong feature.
4. The companion app must be able to produce reports on the posture and the length of duration of the wrong posture and the possible effects of the posture.
5. The device can be a wearable device or a device that can be fixed to other furniture or stuff like that.

CHAPTER SIXTEEN

The Idea: Make a Hair Plaiting machine for women

Difficulty: **Very Difficult**

The Problem: Plaiting a woman's hair into beautiful plaits is one hell of work that every lady is familiar with. Why not make a device to plait the hair instead?

Specifications:

Make a device that will have mechanical actuators that can actually take the hair and plait it into beautiful designs. It can be a handheld device or a fixed apparatus that can be placed on a lady's hair. The machine will scan the head for hair status, fetch the instructions from the companion app in the smartphone and then execute the selected design.

Things to keep in mind:

1. The device must be able to plait several designs.
2. The device should not damage the hair.
3. We must be able to control the device through our smartphones.
4. We must be able to select a design and then execute it on the hair.
5. The device must be able to distinguish between different stages of hair, like plaited, unplaited, straightened, curled, etc.

CHAPTER SEVENTEEN

The Idea: Make a Beard styling machine for men

Difficulty: **Difficult**

The Problem: Speaking of hair, trimming Men's beards as per the latest fashion and trend is no easy task either. We need expert beard stylists for that. Why not make a machine that can not only "cut" the beard, but actually style it as per a selected design?

Specifications:

Make a device that automatically trims men's beards following a selected design through an app on the smartphone. It will be a face machine, that we have to put our face by resting our chin on a pad. Then open the app on your smartphone, choose a beard style, scan and check your face for optimizations and go, you have a smart beard cut.

Things to keep in mind:

1. The device must be able to execute several designs
2. There must be no injury to the face whatsoever
3. There must be a minimum error in executing the design.
4. There must be an auto-stop feature to stop the execution if the machine detects that the person is actually trying to move and get away.
5. The machine must be able to distinguish any half-done or not-done beard styles on human faces.

CHAPTER EIGHTEEN

The Idea: Make a Cat tracking device

Difficulty: **Difficult**

The Problem: Tracking my cat is very difficult, and that too when I am not at home, is almost impossible unless I constantly keep calling someone to know her status.

Specifications:

Make a device that can track my cat and tell me whether she is hungry, what she is possibly doing right now

Things to keep in mind:

1. The device must be able to read my cat's actions such as running hither & thither if she is hungry or not etc.
2. The device must send me her location, especially, if she is not inside the house. Might, if I get a notification, that she is outdoors, will be better.
3. The device will keep track of my cat's health and her vitals, like heartbeats, temperature, etc, and let me know of the records.
4. The device must detect any animal intruder that will possibly fight with here, like a nearby stray dog or something.
5. The device must be connected to the internet through Wi-Fi and I must be able to obtain data through it.

CHAPTER NINETEEN

The Idea: Make a Firewood Dispenser for Fireplace

Difficulty: **Moderate**

The Problem: Stacking Firewood and putting up a Fireplace has never been easy. First, you stack the firewood up in a suitable place, then you manually light the fire, then you put the woods into it, whew, that is a great amount of work, not to mention of all those ash and dirt.

Specifications:

Why not make a mechanical machine that can stack up a pile of firewood and then dispense it to the fireplace with the press of a button? Might be, use electromechanical and programmable systems to do the job?

Things to keep in mind:

1. The machine must be able to store a pile of firewood inside it.
2. Installation of the machine must not mean breaking my old fireplace and making a new one.
3. The firewood could be filled manually, but the user must be notified when the pile is going to be low.
4. It would be great if we could find a way to light that firewood in the fireplace.
5. The machine must not make my fireplace dirty by littering dust, wood fragments or other stuff around.

CHAPTER TWENTY

The Idea: Make a Body massage machine

Difficulty: **Very Difficult**

The Problem: The life of a masseur had never been easy. Providing a good massage needs expertise that can mean visiting a good massage parlor which can be expensive. It is also physically tiresome to provide a good massage.

Specifications:

Why not make a mechanical massaging machine that can actually provide professional massage just like any other masseur? It can be a robotic system that can comprise of a bench with robotic actuation attached to it. A computer can be used to scan a human body and control the actuation to provide a good massage right?

Things to keep in mind:

1. The machine must be able to massage following yogic rules and procedures.
2. There must be options for using oils and other lotions for proper lubrication and relief.
3. There must be an option to only massage a special part of the body, like the head, the legs, the back, the arms, etc
4. The machine must be 100% safe and tested and certified by competent authorities before putting out for sale.
5. Special software must be developed to run the robotic massage system.

CHAPTER TWENTY-ONE

The Idea: Make a Baby diaper assistant device

Difficulty: **Easy**

The Problem: There have been diapers for a while but there is no means to check whether a baby is wet to the fullest or not. Imagine, going to a birthday party with your baby, and you have to keep checking it at regular intervals to make sure, he doesn't cry and worst, not to rush to the bathroom leaving the precious moments aside.

Specifications:

Let's make a baby diaper assistant device that will keep checking the wetness of a baby's diaper and will inform you via your mobile app when to change his diaper and the current status of the diaper.

Things to keep in mind:

1. The device must be small enough to stick into a diaper.
2. The device must be comfortable enough for babies.
3. The device must be safe from all aspects such as electromagnetic radiation, an electrical short circuit inside the device, etc.
4. The device must have its own power source, most probably, from a microcell.
5. We must be able to communicate with the device through an app on our smartphone.

CHAPTER TWENTY-TWO

The Idea: Make a Parcel Delivery System

Difficulty: **Difficult**

The Problem: Imagine, you live on the 30th floor. You have a courier, so the delivery boy will either have to move himself up the 3o floors or if your building has a parcel delivery arrangement, some other person has to pick that up and send it manually to the 30th floor right?

Specifications:

Why not make a "courier lift" just to send parcels up and down high-rise buildings? It will be just like any other lift but with the exception, humans cannot be moved through it. (LOL) It will comprise of carriage belts, robotic actuations, and tracing sensors that will push and pull things up and down the building.

Things to keep in mind:

1. The machine must be able to deliver heavy loads up to 20 kilograms.
2. The machine must be easily installable to any high-rise building.
3. The machine must have sensors to track, which parcel is going where.
4. There must be accompanying software to track and manage the parcel movement and deliveries.
5. The sender and receiver must be intimated once the right person gets the delivery.

CHAPTER TWENTY-THREE

The Idea: Make a Mechanical Dining Table

Difficulty: **Moderate**

The Problem: Have you ever been too large a dining party arrangement? Sitting amidst 20 people or such, you have to be served by other people waiting behind you right? Even with a lesser number of people, moving dishes around the table seems to be a very complicated matter. Someone might need the chicken, while someone might need the Fish Curry!

Specifications:

Make a mechanical dining table so that, the food is served through a revolving system that carries the food around the table. There will be one touch screen display device each attached to every seat and a routing mechanism that will keep the food moving around. You pick what you want from the menu on the display, and a smart algorithm will route the dish to your side the quickest way possible.

Things to keep in mind:

1. The machine must be able to handle solid and fluids alike.
2. There might be as many as 20 dishes on the table.
3. The smallest table might have 3 seats and the largest might have 30.
4. There must be some algorithm to decide which way is the quickest.
5. The machine must not spill curry to your suit.

CHAPTER TWENTY-FOUR

The Idea: Make a Back-scrubber device for the bathroom

Difficulty: **Simple**

The Problem: How do you scrub your back in the bathroom? I find it very difficult, and sometimes I really do skip scrubbing my back using the stupid scrubber with the handle.

Specifications:

Make a mechanical back scrubber that can effectively scrub and clean my back while I am bathing. I must also be able to use it for my arms, thighs, and buttocks too.

Things to keep in mind:

1. The machine must be waterproof (very clear)
2. The machine must be soft enough to use on a human body.
3. The machine must have an extensible handle with a proper grip, so that, I can extend it or shorten it at my will.
4. The machine must be small enough to be stored in a bathroom closet.
5. The machine must have a rechargeable battery with a charge indicator, all waterproof.

CHAPTER TWENTY-FIVE

The Idea: Make a Window plant Monitoring Device

Difficulty: **Moderate**

The Problem: How do you keep track of your dear money plant while you are on vacation? How do you water it? How do you put it to sunshine or shield it from the sun?

Specifications:

Make a mechanical Window Plants monitoring and management device for my Plants. The machine will have a rack to put my pots upon. It will also have a facility of using water from the hose or using water from a custom tank. It will have blinds on it that it can use to provide shade or sunlight as and when required. All these will be done automatically, and I will be kept informed.

Things to keep in mind:

1. The machine must be fully automatic.
2. The machine must have a camera since I want to see my plants.
3. The machine must water the plants only when required, so it needs to detect when to water.
4. The machine must set the sun-blinds only and when required. As like the watering issue, this must be detected as well.
5. I must have an app on my phone, that I will use to see the plants and monitor their health and growth.

CHAPTER TWENTY-SIX

The Idea: make a Study Tracker for Kids

Difficulty: **Very Difficult**

The Problem: How do I know that my child is actually studying his (physical) textbook or not? Might be, he is lying to me that he is actually studying Chapter No 5. How do I know? Go and check him? Make a robotic spy instead.

Specifications:

Make a device that I will stick to my child's book or stick to his study table and instruct him to study. So, the device will keep tracking what my child is doing, whether he is actually studying or not, if he is, then which is the chapter that he is studying. Might be, the device is artificially intelligent and will track my child's body movements, his eye movements, his lip movements, his hand movements, and also scan the book for information and let me know what he is doing.

Things to keep in mind:

1. The machine must be artificially intelligent
2. The machine must have visual perceptions
3. The machine must be able to scan books he is studying and the information contained in the book, like Book name, Chapter Title, etc.
4. The machine can be communicated through a PC or a smartphone.
5. The machine must be able to send sufficient data for exhaustive statistics.

CHAPTER TWENTY-SEVEN

The Idea: Make a Fish Processor machine

Difficulty: **Difficult**

The Problem: When you buy uncut fresh fish from the market or catch some by yourself, how do you process it? Cleaning scales, then cutting it up, removing its interiors, etc. The job is messy and difficult for the inexperienced.

Specifications:

Make a fish scales removal device with a feature to cut and clean the fish into neat pieces. Put the fish one way into a machine that will have robotic grippers and rotating actuators that will remove the scales. The system will then use water to flush out the junk to a container and then, cut the fish as per instructions to get pieces of fish meat in a collecting bowl.

Things to keep in mind:

1. The machine must have a display that will show options to process the fish, like the sizes you want, whether to keep it wholesome or not etc.
2. The machine will have adjustable blades that will cut the fish in a variety of sizes as per the instructions entered into the machine.
3. The machine will have an internal container to collect the waste material.
4. The machine will use water from our kitchen hose to flush garbage from the fish.
5. Finally, the machine will dispense meat into a bowl.

CHAPTER TWENTY-EIGHT

The Idea: Bio-Gas Stove from Cow Dung

Difficulty: **Moderate**

The Problem: Cow Dung is manure, but in many ways, it turns out to be a waste frequently. With a low amount of cow dung, conventional Bio Gas collection systems are inefficient. How do we make use of lesser quantities of Cow Dung to get flammable Bio Gas?

Specifications:

Create an ingenious way of getting Bio Gas from very less amount of Cow Dung or similar stuff. Make an outdoor device with pipes going to the kitchen. Put a digital monitoring system to track gas production and gas pressure.

Things to keep in mind:

1. The machine must be strong enough to withstand gas pressures.
2. The machine must have the ability to generate Bio Gas from lesser amounts of dung which will be useful for small households.
3. The machine must have a self-cleaning system that will help the owner to clean it.
4. We must be able to monitor the functioning of the system through digital systems.
5. The system must be safe from every aspect like Gas Leakages and Pressure faults.

CHAPTER TWENTY-NINE

The Idea: Make a Retractable shelf

Difficulty: **Simple**

The Problem: How do you fetch things from tall shelves? Especially, books from tall racks and kitchen stuff from tall cupboards overhead? Use a ladder?

Specifications:

Design a retractable shelf that has a foldable top that brings the closet down to reach on the press of a switch. The entire shelf structure will have robotic actuators that assist in moving cupboards and closets along with their contents to the user's reach when the desired closet number is pressed on the keypad beside the shelf.

Things to keep in mind:

1. The machine must be strong enough to handle weights up to 44 pounds (or around 20 kilograms)
2. The contents must not be disturbed in any way that may include, spilling and breakage.
3. The machine must run on a domestic power supply and must consume as minimum electricity as possible.
4. The same retractable feature can be used for closets down below which are harder to reach for persons having low back pain and for senior people.
5. It would be better if we could make a software to record, what things are in which closet.

CHAPTER THIRTY

The Idea: Artificially Intelligent CCTV surveillance system

Difficulty: **Difficult**

The Problem: A customer whisks his gun up to your forehead and asks for the cash. How come, you didn't notice, that he was the bad guy with vile intentions?

Specifications:

Make a smart CCTV surveillance system that is powered by Artificial Intelligence and Machine Learning algorithms. The system will scan for every person in the vicinity for possible features of the 'Bad-Guy'. Try to find out if they might have something up their sleeve or something. Might be, the Police can provide some sort of API service for public consumption which lets you match profiles of suspects with established criminal profiles from databases sources through Police Intelligence.

Things to keep in mind:

1. The device must be capable of reading human body language and facial features.
2. There can be supporting systems such as metal detectors etc that can feed data to the system.
3. There can be external cameras that can track and read vehicles and their license plates.
4. There must be some sort of alarm system that cleverly alerts the Business owner, people managing the business at that moment, and the Police.
5. The device must make sure, it doesn't mess up the security of the people in general.

CHAPTER THIRTY-ONE

The Idea: Make a Smart Pest Scanner for homes

Difficulty: **Difficult**

The Problem: You enter the washroom and find a large snake in the sink. How could you know, that something has entered the house while you were sleeping?

Specifications:

Make a smart pest surveillance system that scans every nook and corner of the house through intelligent scanning systems that is powered by AI and ML. The system will look for household pests and other animals that might enter the house and pose a threat. The device must be suitable for use in homes, restaurants, malls, offices, etc.

Things to keep in mind:

1. The device must be capable of making the difference between a Dog and a Coyote.
2. The device can have assistive sensing in the form of odor sensor and preceptory sensing through CCTV.
3. The system must sound an alarm and send a notification to the homeowners once a threat is detected.
4. The system must be capable of connecting to the internet and sending notifications to owners who might be away on a trip.
5. There might be an optional arrangement of notifying the animal rescue department in case a possible threat is identified.

CHAPTER THIRTY-TWO

The Idea: Make a Smart Speed Monitoring Sensor network

Difficulty: **Difficult**

The Problem: Millions of people die every year due to speeding and losing control of their vehicles. The Police have always struggled to curb this and save human lives.

Specifications:

Create a smart speed monitoring sensor network that can be fitted to every vehicle and then can track the speed of the vehicle with respect to the speed limit permitted in the area and in the case of overspeeding, notify the driver and lower the speed automatically. In case, the driver overrides this alarm, he will be issued a digital speeding ticket automatically.

Things to keep in mind:

1. The system must be able to get information regarding the highway and the permitted speed on that road. So, we will need a network of systems plugged in together.
2. The driver of the vehicle might be able to bypass the warning and alarms in case of an emergency that he deems fit to be overridden. He might have to prove this emergency in court to avoid the ticket.
3. Every vehicle with this device will be connected to a cloud network, that will be assisted with GPS.
4. The location and speed range data can be obtained from cloud servers.
5. The Police can get this information in Real-Time from the cloud.

CHAPTER THIRTY-THREE

The Idea: Make a Dog assistant device

Difficulty: **VeryDifficult**

The Problem: I had to go on a business trip and I had the leave my dog with my neighbor who is not that good at dealing with dogs, especially, he has no experience when to do what with the cute little things.

Specifications:

Make a device to attach to the collar of my doggie so that it finds out why he is barking, why is he wagging his tail so much or why is he pulling at my skirt. The device is an intelligent piece of machinery that translates the actions of the dog through an accompanying app and lets even the novice user understand doggie behavior.

Things to keep in mind:

1. The device must be tiny enough to be attached to a dog collar.
2. The device must give its power source and must be connected to an app on my mobile.
3. The device must track the dog's actions and process the best corresponding meanings for the user and what actions the user is now supposed to do.
4. It will be better if the device can also monitor my dog's vitals such as body temperature and heart rate.
5. The device must be able to produce statistical reports that say about the behavioral pattern and health of my dog.

CHAPTER THIRTY-FOUR

The Idea: Cloth Cutting Machine – Tailor Assistant

Difficulty: **Moderate**

The Problem: I am a fashion designer and I have to cut the cloth according to predefined patterns and as per calculated dimensions. This is a very intricate job and is very difficult to do too. One small mistake, and the cloth is good for the dustbin.

Specifications:

Make a machine that will cut raw pieces of cloth into designs and patterns I want. The machine will have a display connected to it and will have a menu. I will choose my design from the offered designs and set the dimensions and put the cloth into the die just as I put paper into my printer. On a execute button press, the machine will cut the cloth as required.

Things to keep in mind:

1. The device must be able to cut cloth exactly as per measurements, not a centimeter here or a centimeter there.
2. The device must cut cloth in such a manner that wastage of cloth is minimized.
3. We must be able to download new designs into the machine.
4. We must be able to cut into multiple layers of cloth.
5. It would be great if we can have a mobile app for the machine.

CHAPTER THIRTY-FIVE

The Idea: Make an Electronic Greenhouse Tube for nurseries

Difficulty: **Difficult**

The Problem: It is very difficult to maintain climatic conditions for nurseries to grow plants. One set of plants would need 25°C to grow whereas another set of plants in the nursery would require 35°C to grow properly. Also, maintaining humidity and water flow is difficult too.

Specifications:

Make a circular large tube-like structure that can house several saplings and the tube will be digitally controlled for temperature, humidity, and water.

Things to keep in mind:

1. The machine must be fully controllable through a computer that will help regulate the vital elements of the Greenhouse tube.
2. We must be able to supply, heat, water, and other necessary elements to the tube through some proper mechanism.
3. We must be able to run the machine without hampering other vegetation nearby.
4. The machine must have the capability to sense the inner and exterior of the tube and then adjust the climatic conditions accordingly.
5. The machine must have software that must track the climatic conditions and produce statistical reports

CHAPTER THIRTY-SIX

The Idea: Make a Facial Makeup Machine for ladies

Difficulty: **Very Difficult**

The Problem: Ladies will understand what's the issue with doing makeup. It might be something from a simple to a very elaborate process with quite a level of expertise needed to produce the desired effect. It is also time-consuming and tiresome.

Specifications:

Design a machine for ladies that will have a turntable to place their faces in and a scanner will scan their faces for exact dimensions and contours. From a selected makeup procedure, execute the process with the help of mechanical actuators and through makeup material stores into the machine. This might be something similar to the beard trimming machine for men.

Things to keep in mind:

1. The machine will have a display device that will provide a menu to choose styles from.
2. The machine will have containers for materials, that it will sense, just as a printer senses the ink levels.
3. The machine must be able to do eye and lips too, which is as difficult as hell.
4. The machine has to provide levels of exposure as required that might include different styling parameters.
5. The machine must be able to execute highlights too with blends as white, pinkish, reddish, etc.

CHAPTER THIRTY-SEVEN

The Idea: Make a Wall and Ceiling cleaning machine

Difficulty: **Very Difficult**

The Problem: I have a machine to clean the floors of my room. But, how to clean the walls and ceiling of my room?

Specifications:

Create a robotic machine to clean the Walls and Ceilings of my house and collect the garbage in a bin just like the vacuum cleaner. Make sure, the machine doesn't dislodge things hung on the walls and ceiling.

Things to keep in mind:

1. The machine must be able to climb the walls and ceilings without falling off on someone's head.
2. The machine must be able to detect and overcome any obstacles such as paintings, cupboards, drawers, ceiling fans, air-conditioners, etc.
3. The machine must not peel off any wallpaper during the cleaning process.
4. The machine must not spill dust and other garbage here and there.
5. There must be a suitable power supply or an ingenious way of powering the device so that it doesn't come in the way of the machine or any other objects in the room which might lead to disaster.

CHAPTER THIRTY-EIGHT

The Idea: Make a Bed making machine

Difficulty: **Difficult**

The Problem: I have returned from a hard day at work and having some fun at a party, I am tired and I don't want to make and arrange my bed for sleep. How I wish, there had been a machine to make the bed for me.

Specifications:

Make a machine that will make my bed by either making it ready for sleep or arranging it back to order in the morning. It will have a container for storing bedspreads, covers, quilts, pillows, etc. On the switch of a button, my bed will be ready by itself. The machine can be robotic arm-based or X-Y Rails system or something.

Things to keep in mind:

1. The machine must be able to remove one bedsheet and put another. The same goes for pillows.
2. The machine must be able to clean and dust the bed.
3. The machine must have storage for my bedsheets, covers, blankets, pillows, that it will arrange on the bed for me.
4. The machine must also be able to clean the bed in the morning and put it back to order. Things that may require further washing must be put aside in a different bin.
5. Detection of the status of the bed like arranged/not arranged or clean/dirty must be detected by the machine.

CHAPTER THIRTY-NINE

The Idea: Make a Shit Cleaning Machine for the elderly

Difficulty: **Difficult**

The Problem: My 91-year-old Mom needs assistance every day going to the bathroom. She has sitting difficulty in the bathroom and I have to help her sit and get up, and worse, she cannot clean herself up. Now, I have to go on a business trip overseas and I have to appoint a nurse to take care of her.

Specifications:

Make a smart machine that will clean the shit of my Mom's ass with the click of a button. Wipe it, clean it and discard the tissue out into a disposable can, all automatically. That way, other people have an easy time assisting the elderly.

Things to keep in mind:

1. The machine must be able to clean the shit of a person sitting on the commode or a person sleeping on the bed.
2. The machine must be able to use both tissue paper and or water to do the job.
3. The waste materials must be collected in a disposable container that can be later discarded.
4. The machine must be safe and hygienic for daily use.
5. The machine must be portable enough so that it can be easily moved from one place to another.

CHAPTER FORTY

The Idea: Make a Tie Knot Machine

Difficulty: **Moderate**

The Problem: Knotting my tie properly needs a few moments and required some expertise too. Also, I find it difficult to tie the know in a fancy way that I saw on the internet.

Specifications:

Make a smart machine that will tie knots for my tie around my neck. There will be a display device, possibly connected to my smartphone. There will be an interface presenting me with several styles for Tie Knots. Once I select a style, the machine will look for a tie in a slot and then execute the design on my tie.

Things to keep in mind:

1. The machine must be able to tie the knot quickly, faster than a human, else it will not be feasible to own such as machine.
2. The machine must be able to tie a knot, both around a neck and without a person in it.
3. The machine must be able to tie different designs of tie knots.
4. Different styles must be available in the app and that can be used in the device.
5. The machine must be capable of resolving a knot too.

CHAPTER FORTY-ONE

The Idea: Make an Omelette frying Machine

Difficulty: **Simple**

The Problem: I want to quickly make an Omelette and that too, in a different style. I need a custom shape with a custom recipe that I saw on YouTube. I want the machine to fry the Omelette for me.

Specifications:

Design an Omelette making machine that can process eggs following a certain recipe, and fry an Omelette. There will be containers for ingredients such as Onion, Chilly, Garlic, Turmeric, Coriander, etc. The device will have a display with a menu and will present me with different recipes and allow me to fill the containers with chopped pieces of the ingredients required. Once ready, it will fry Omelette for me in the quantities I need.

Things to keep in mind:

1. The machine must be able to store raw ingredients temporarily before executing the fry.
2. The machine must have different frying designs, like Circular, Oval, Heart Shaped, Star Shaped, etc.
3. The machine must be able to follow pre-defined recipes and produce yummy results.
4. Make sure, the Omelette is not burnt down in the process.
5. The user must be notified after the job is done.

CHAPTER FORTY-TWO

The Idea: Make a Geo Fence for Kids

Difficulty: **Difficult**

The Problem: My 4-year-old kid keeps going here and there and often visits me in my barn where I have my machine workshop. Sometimes, I don't even have the slightest clue that he is there. On other occasions, he would just veer off close to the nearby pool, unless someone keeps a strict vigil on him all the time.

Specifications:

Design a Geo-Fencing system that monitors my kid's movements. It will have multiple sensing nodes and will be connected through Wi-Fi. I will have the option of defining which areas are dangerous for my kid to enter or be close by and I will strap some tracking device to my kid's clothing. The system will keep monitoring where he is going and what he is trying to do. It will sound an alarm and also notify me in case it senses any danger.

Things to keep in mind:

1. I must be able to define areas inside my campus as very dangerous, moderately dangerous, etc.
2. The whole network must work in coordination.
3. The system must have a backup power source or must have the option of getting power from UPS Services in my home.
4. The system must have a central alarm system.
5. I must be notified via my phone, what exactly is the location of my kid.

CHAPTER FORTY-THREE

The Idea: Make a Hair Comb Cleaning Device

Difficulty: **Simple**

The Problem: I have to wash my hair combs almost every single day, because my hair is falling out, and I have got dandruff too. While the treatment is going on, I hate to wash the combs in the basin.

Specifications:

Make a hair comb cleaning machine that is quite similar to a washing machine and one that will get rid of manually cleaning those. It will be a simple machine with a jar to put my combs in. I will have the option to put in cleaning agents or detergents and with the push of a button, all my hair combs will be cleaned as new.

Things to keep in mind:

1. The machine must be able to clean even the thickest of combs and the densest of combs.
2. I must be able to wash my combs one by one, as a single piece or all of those together,
3. The machine might use water just like a washing machine does.
4. The waste material must be either collected in a bin or put through a hose, just like a washing machine.
5. The machine must be portable enough to carry in a small bag during my trip.

CHAPTER FORTY-FOUR

The Idea: Make an Indian Henna Machine

Difficulty: **VeryDifficult**

The Problem: One who has done Henna (Mehndi) on his body, especially on their palms, have realized, how difficult the job is. It requires great balance, skill, expertise, and creativity to carry out one of such designs and thus, are very expensive things to be done.

Specifications:

Create an Indian Henna machine that can print beautiful designs on a person's body parts, such as palms, arms, legs, etc. There will be a container to store the henna. Some sort of articulated actuation system will then make the designs as per selection done through a visual interface.

Things to keep in mind:

1. The machine must be able to print out different designs and patterns.
2. Make sure the machine doesn't spill henna here and there.
3. The machine must be able to communicate with an app on my smartphone so that I can select a design.
4. The machine must be able to print in both thin and thick lines.
5. It will be better if the machine can make designs not only on palms but also on arms and legs.

CHAPTER FORTY-FIVE

The Idea: Make a Roof Cleaning Machine

Difficulty: **Moderate**

The Problem: It is very cumbersome to clean the roof of my house. My roof very frequently collects garbage on top in the form of dust, dead leaves, and all other stuff. I want to keep it as clean as new all the time.

Specifications:

Make a roof cleaning device that can clean the roof of houses without someone actually climbing onto the top of it. The machine will have some sort of framework that will support the actual cleaning device. I will let the device scan my roof and then provide me with options to clean it.

Things to keep in mind:

1. The machine must be able to clean a wide variety of roofs from concrete to tiles.
2. The machine must get itself up to the roof instead of someone climbing the terrace and putting it over it.
3. The machine must be able to scan and process roof data through sensors and provide that to the user through some sort of interface.
4. The machine must be able to use water, detergent and other cleaning agents to wash and clean the roof.
5. The machine must be possibly waterproof to avoid technical damage to itself.

CHAPTER FORTY-SIX

The Idea: Make a Kid monitor for Cars

Difficulty: **Moderate**

The Problem: I have three kids and whenever I drive, two of them create a ruckus on the backseat and keep doing things that I don't allow them to do. The third one is my 18-month-old baby whom I strap to the baby seat on the backseat. She keeps jeering left and right with every turn and I being a mom, hardly can concentrate on my driving with all of them in my backseat.

Specifications:

Create a kid monitoring device that will keep a strict eye on my kids and keeps warning them from doing things that they are not supposed to do and also keeps me informed without me having to look back or the mirror for the naughty kids. Also, a baby monitor that checks if my baby is alright or not will be of great help.

Things to keep in mind:

1. It must be easy to install the device in most cars.
2. The device must have artificially intelligent sensing and tracking algorithms that can find out what is happening in the backseat and map those out to a predefined set of actions.
3. The device must play audible instructions as warnings for kids and also notifications for the driver that something might not be right, and she needs to stop.
4. The device must also have a camera attached to it.
5. Make sure, the device is a life-saving instrument.

CHAPTER FORTY-SEVEN

The Idea: Make a Coconut Scraping Machine

Difficulty: **Simple**

The Problem: I have a coconut tree in my garden and it bears sweet coconuts for me. I saw a dish on YouTube and I need to get the coconut white as scraped dust. How do I do that?

Specifications:

Make a machine to clean coconut and scrape it for the whites and collect it in a bowl. The machine must have a place to put a bowl. I will then attach the count to some actuation mechanism. The machine will have some sort of scanning mechanism that, on the press of the execute button, will first find out the thickness of the white matter and then, process the extraction of the white matter.

Things to keep in mind:

1. The machine must be able to remove the hard layers of the coconut.
2. It must also be able to scrape the coconut for the white material and then collect it in a bowl.
3. The machine must not damage the coconut while performing the scarping.
4. The brownish shell must not be scraped while trying to get the whites.
5. Also, the whites must be extracted as much as possible.

CHAPTER FORTY-EIGHT

The Idea: Make a Grey Beard Hair plucking Device for men

Difficulty: **Very Difficult**

The Problem: I am greying and I keep a beard. I find it very ugly to have strands of grey beard hanging here and there and I spend a lot of time trying to whisk them off my beard with a pair of scissors. It's cumbersome, tiresome, time-consuming, and boring.

Specifications:

Devise a machine to pluck all those grey hair out from the beard. The machine will have a face mask, I will put my face to it. It will then scan my face for grey hair and, through some sort of ingenious mechanical actuation, the great machine will pluck those silly grey beard hair off my face.

Things to keep in mind:

1. The machine must be able to scan my face for grey hair.
2. It must be able to distinguish between grey and black hair.
3. I might have a colored beard, make sure, it doesn't pluck of black or other colored hair, only the grey ones.
4. Make sure, the plucked off hair is not littered anywhere, I want those to be collected in some sort of container.
5. It must be safe for my face in all respects.

CHAPTER FORTY-NINE

The Idea: Make a Walking Exoskeleton for the disabled

Difficulty: **Very Difficult**

The Problem: My cousin met with an unfortunate accident several years ago and both of his legs had to be amputated. Now he uses, artificial legs to move around and sometimes an electric wheelchair. The artificial legs are no good, and he describes them to be clumsy and unresponsive.

Specifications:

Make a machine that will be like an exoskeleton having two robotic human legs. Once inside it, the robotic legs will do the walking for him. The machine might get the reflex sensing from the thigh muscles or from nerve endings that come from the brain.

Things to keep in mind:

1. Make sure, my brother doesn't wander away hundreds of miles away without wanting to go anyway.
2. Make sure, the robotic exoskeleton gets the proper and correct signals to perform the walking.
3. Put a manual control system in case something goes wrong and he wants it otherwise.
4. The device must have its own rechargeable power supply too.
5. The device must be lightweight, efficient, and responsive toward human reflexes.

CHAPTER FIFTY

The Idea: Make an Electro-mechanical office organizer closet

Difficulty: **Moderate**

The Problem: Have you seen my office table? It's good, you haven't. All the things are littered around like hell, and to make things worse, I can't find things on time. I spend hours on weekends cleaning and arranging things like files, diaries, staplers, pens, pins, paper, visiting cards, and the like.

Specifications:

Create a mechanical closet that can store all the office stationery including files, diaries, visiting cards, etc. it will have compartments and a display that provides an interface to put things inside with identifying names. With the click of a switch from a menu, the closet will fetch that item from storage.

Things to keep in mind:

1. The closet must be compact and easily instable to an average office desk.
2. It must have a mechanism to identify which item is stored in which container.
3. All the items must be produced through the same outlet and again must be stored mechanically into their original housing.
4. The machine must have its own software to store and manage the items inside it,
5. The machine must produce records of items inside it and display them through the interface.

Copyrights

What you can do: copy ideas from this book and use them in your projects as your own. Apply for patents based on ideas from this book, improve those ideas and then claim for patents.

What you cannot do: you cannot copy any content from this book, put it in another publication, physically or digitally, as image or text, and claim as your own creation or resell parts of this book without the author's prior written permission.

For copyright licenses:
victorborah@gmail.com
First Published: **2022**
Published By: **Victor Vashkar Borah**
For copyright licenses:
victorborah@gmail.com

Printed by Libri Plureos GmbH in Hamburg,
Germany